A Child's Portrait of Shakespeare

by

Lois Burdett

FIREFLY BOOKS

A FIREFLY BOOK

Published by Firefly Books Ltd.

Copyright © 1995 Lois Burdett

Sixth Printing, 2009

First published in April, 1995 by Black Moss Press
with the assistance of the Canada Council and the
Ontario Arts Council and the Department of
Canada Heritage.

Canadian Cataloguing in Publication Data
Burdett, Lois, 1950
(Shakespeare can be fun)
ISBN-13: 978-0-88753-263-4 (bound)
ISBN-10: 0-88753-263-2 (bound)
ISBN-13: 978-0-88753-261-0 (pbk.)
ISBN-10: 0-88753-261-6 (pbk.)
1. Shakespeare, William, 1564-1616—
Biography—Juvenile literature.
2. Dramatists, English—Early modern,
1500-1700—Biography—Juvenile literature.
I. Title. II. Series
PR2895.B87 1995   j822.3'3   C95-900228-6

Published in Canada by
Firefly Books Ltd.
66 Leek Crescent
Richmond Hill, Ontario
L4B 1H1

Published in the United States by
Firefly Books (U.S.) Inc.
P.O. Box 1338, Ellicott Station
Buffalo, New York 14205

Design concept by Lois Burdett
Manufactured by Friesens in Altona, Manitoba,
Canada in September, 2009, Job# 50363

Jennifer Hoke (age 8

Front Cover: Julia Graham (age 8)
Title Page: Adam Robinson (age 8)
Back Cover: Kate Bean (age 7), Andrea Bardens (age 7)

*The Publisher acknowledges the financial support of the
Government of Canada through the Book Publishing Industry
Development Program for our publishing activities.*

Other books in the series:
Twelfth Night for Kids
Macbeth for Kids
A Midsummer Night's Dream for Kids
Romeo and Juliet for Kids
The Tempest for Kids
Much Ado About Nothing for Kids

Foreword

When my daughter was a little girl, I used to tell her bedtime stories, once she was hunkered down and ready to go to sleep. As my original story-telling skills are negligible, I would borrow from any source I could think of, often from the plays I was rehearsing at the time.

The plays of Shakespeare proved to be particularly interesting story-telling material for her, from the age of three on. One of the first to grace her imagination was the (somewhat truncated) story of Hamlet, which as I remember started something like this:

"Once upon a time, there was a young prince named Hamlet. Poor Hamlet's father died and Hamlet's mother married his Uncle Claudius and that made Hamlet VEEEERRRRRRRRRY ANGRY!"

She is now a couple of decades older than three, but her interest in Shakespeare and her lack of intimidation about these great plays has served her well through many years of schooling and theatre-going. It is to my great regret that she never had Lois Burdett as a teacher.

Lois Burdett has done the same thing and much, much more for a generation of youngsters since she first had the vision to teach Shakespeare to her grade two and three students in a form that they found interesting and fun. She makes them participants in these timeless stories, allows them to create subtext and background, flesh out characterizations in their own way and invent dialogue that suits the events. It's clear by the material in *A Child's Portrait of Shakespeare* that she invites them to know Shakespeare as if he were a live playwright—indeed, a friend.

The first time I attended one of Mrs. Burdett's classes, I was astounded by the vigour and excitement the kids felt being a part of the Shakespeare project. They couldn't wait to tell me what Olivia was really thinking or what terrible pain Sebastian went through trying to find his long-lost sister. They had gotten inside the skin of the characters in Twelfth Night in a way that most actors spend months trying to achieve.

Their "versions" of the plays are enchanting, moving and very, very funny. They are also astonishingly accurate. And these children grow up with one of the greatest geniuses of all time inside their skins and brains. Would that all education was as fruitful, as creative, as useful, in our adult lives.

A Child's Portrait of Shakespeare is the next evolution (after the Twelfth Night book) of these students' intimacy with Shakespeare; here they explore the man and the time in which he lived. Every educator, every parent, every child should own these records of classes of children who love school and learning and who, through Lois Burdett's own genius, feel that Shakespeare belongs to them.

Martha Henry
Stratford, Ontario, Canada

It has been my privilege over the past 20 years to teach Grade 2 and 3 students at Hamlet Public School in Stratford, Ontario. These children brought to the classroom fertile minds and a desire to learn. Together, we explored the magic of Shakespeare. Their words and art took on a dramatic quality and revealed a freshness that comes from the very young. I dedicate this book to all of these students.

-Lois Burdett

Who is William Shakespeare?

I asked my seven and eight year old students.
Their answers were surprising.

William Shakespeare?
Isn't he the President of Canada?

No way!
He's just an old timer!

I think I know...
Maybe Tammy's brother.

Well, he's sure not my brother.
I don't even have a brother.

I don't know who he is...
I don't know any of the big kids.

The whole class became detectives. We looked at pictures and read historic accounts of the Bard. I guided the search, but let the children have the freedom to imagine themselves back in Shakespeare's time. They were soon living the part and were so absorbed that in their imaginations, they became Shakespeare.

But let their unedited work speak for itself!

On a day that was just like today, but many years ago,
A boy was born in England who we think you all should know.

This lad grew up to write a lot of bright and famous plays;
Ideas that consumed his mind could fill up many days.

Marijke Altenburg
(age 7)

Now, can you guess the name of this important writing man?
Of course, it's William Shakespeare! We will tell you all we can.

Romeo and Juliet

A Midsummer Night's Dream

Tyler Preston (age 7)

Robyn Lafontaine (age 7)

Julius Caesar

Adam Robinson (age 8)

The first part of our story is of where Will started from,
So maybe we should let you know about his Dad and Mom.

John Shakespeare was a glover and a wool dealer you see;
He made a decent living; things were happy as could be.

Mary Arden was his wife, a local farmer's daughter;
She lived with John on Henley Street, content with all life brought her.

*Ashley Kropf,
(age 9)*

John Shakespeare

Mary Arden

They were respected citizens and lived in style and grace
In Stratford-upon-Avon, near a busy marketplace.

Henley Street
Stratford-upon-Avon

Jenny Geoghegan (age 8)

On April 23, while light was fading from the sky,
The silent air was shattered by a baby's lusty cry.

The infant was the family's third; the first two girls met death,
So William was an only child when drawing his first breath.

Courtney Chadwick,
(age 7)

April 23, 1564

Dear Diary,
It was at night that I herd it, the sound I had been waiting for... A new baby, my very own. My hart grew and grew. His eyes winked in the candle light and his cheeks were as soft as dove fethers. He was kom and quiet. Then a name shot into my head and I shouted WILLIAM SHAKESPEARE! Mary and I danced around the room. Probly all Henley Street was awake. We had a big selebrashin!

John Shakespeare

Alex Woodley (age 8)

His parents could not comprehend when gazing down with glee,
That little William was to be a writing prodigy.

John Shakespeare   Mary Arden

Kimberly Brown (age 8)

Three days later at a church, the tiny tot was christened;
Small William was anointed while his parents watched and listened.

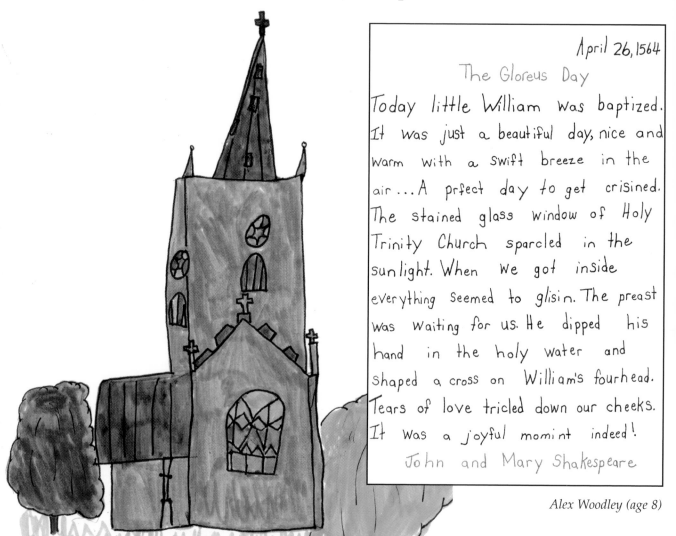

April 26, 1564

The Gloreus Day

Today little William was baptized. It was just a beautiful day, nice and warm with a swift breeze in the air ... A prfect day to get crisined. The stained glass window of Holy Trinity Church sparcled in the sunlight. When we got inside everything seemed to glisin. The preast was waiting for us. He dipped his hand in the holy water and shaped a cross on William's fourhead. Tears of love tricled down our cheeks. It was a joyful momint indeed! John and Mary Shakespeare

Alex Woodley (age 8)

Anika Johnson (age 7)

Holy Trinity Church

John was weak with happiness as he looked upon his boy,
His sweet and tiny infant was a source of utter joy.

And Mary's heart was leaping as she held her baby near;
His sounds of soft contentment were a ballad to her ear.

Brittany Shaw
(age 7)

13

But times were not quite perfect in those first few days of life,
For William was a normal child who caused his Mom some strife.

His cries were loud and constant through the minutes of the night;
Poor Mary mourned her missing sleep and William's appetite.

MARY ARDEN'S DIARY

Dear Diary 1564 April 28

I have a spliting headacke. William just won't fall asleep! I sang him a lulaby but he just screems all the louder. I forgot how hard it was having a baby. All night little William cried. I wonder what he is going to be when he grows up... a sailer, a wrighter?

Oh never mind

I'm going to sleep!

Lauren Gr. 2

Mary Arden

Courtney Chadwick (age 7)

Lauren Vancea (age 7)

14

Now William grew robust and strong, avoiding the Black Death
Which killed so many babies, taking life with one cold breath.

The Black Plague

The Black Plague is a <u>horible</u> disees. If you took Europe and divided it in four, a quarter of the people would have died. But what the people <u>didn't</u> know is that the Black Plague is caused by rats. Rats give it to the fleas. Then the fleas bite the people. Things were not as clean back then. The people just dumped their garbage out the window, and they didn't have the tylinol or anteebyotics to cure the problem.

Story: Katie Brown (age 7)
Art: Sophie Jones (age 7)

Will's childhood days were happy and four years quickly passed,
He seemed to have good fortune that was always going to last.

His Dad had been appointed to a job of some renown;
His title was High Bailiff or the Mayor of their town.

Dulcie
Vousden
(age 7)

John Shakespeare
The Mayor of Stratford

All these counsel meetings can be very tiring. I hardly get to spend any time with William. He wants to play with me every morning. I hate to disapoynt him but my job is important to me and with another mouth to feed we do need more muney. Mary is up to her ears in house chores so I hardly even get to see her. I think we are in for some very bisy years.

John Shakespeare

Glenn Truelove (age 7)

16

But what did William do all day? It's hard for us, you see,
To visualize a time without Nintendo or TV.

There were no movie cinemas or arcades to enthrall;
In fact, we must state here, there were no theatres at all.

Back then, the actors roamed in carts to show the people plays;
They set up in a local square and worked for several days.

Alex Woodley (age 8)

It must have been exciting in the year that Will was five
When the players of the Queen at his village did arrive.

Alex Woodley
(age 8)

Ella Fox (age 7)

11:00 A.M. Saturday
June 3 ,1568

I am so exsited I think I will explode. Today
The Queen's Player's are coming to town. Dad
said if I'm good I can come too. I put on my
best clothes and waited at the window. Finally I
herd the sound of trumpits. The drums were
rolling and I could see their wagon in the distens
All the sitizens of Stratford started to clap and
cheer.
William

And little Will rushed out to watch the Queen's men by their wagon;
He sat in rapture while they put on St. George and the Dragon.

John paid them all nine shillings for their work upon that day.
Then they gathered up their costumes and went on their merry way.

Adam Robinson (age 8)

When Will turned six or seven, he was sent to grammar school;
He had to study hard because the punishments were cruel.

The days were long and tiring; they began at early dawn.
They lasted 'til late afternoon when light was almost gone.

Dulcie Vousden
(age 7)

I have to get up at five o'clock in the morning to get to my gramer school by six. What a bumer! My school doesn't end until five o'clock at night. I am eggzosted by the end of the day!

William Shakespeare

Amberly Henry (age 7)

Will studied hard at Latin, geometry and Greek.
He also read the Bible in the schoolroom, which was bleak.

Now girls of William's age were not permitted to attend;
They had to stay at home to help with housework and to mend.

Dulcie Vousden (age 7)

I definitly would <u>not</u> I mean <u>not</u> want to go to school in Shakespeare's time. All that Latin and Greek would make my eyes tired!
Ella

Ella Fox (age 7)

When William was fourteen, his father had a lot of trouble.
It seemed within a year or two, his life had turned to rubble.

Kyle Jones
(age 7)

22

For John was deep in debt, which had amounted over time.
He never went to church which was considered then a crime.

He missed his council meetings and he mortgaged his estate.
He couldn't pay his taxes and his bills were often late.

John
Shakespeare
1578

*Alison Dickens
(age 8)*

Ella Fox (age 7)

There never seems to be enuf muney. My family is skared to death! I am trying to settle everyone down but it is much too frightuning. There just doesn't seem to be anyway out of this.

But William still survived this mess and grew to be eighteen;
Then a pretty girl, Anne Hathaway, arrived upon the scene.

Kris Murray
(age 7)

Anne Hathaways Cottage

Jenny Geoghegan (age 8)

'Twas quite a walk to ask her out, we think you will agree,
For she lived about a mile away in nearby Shottery.

We call her home the cottage now and it is full of charm,
But back when Anne was living there, the name was Hewlands Farm.

The Bard pursued her gallantly with letters of devotion;
He knew this love was more than just a silly passing notion.

Dear Annie,
Would you like to go on a date with me? If you would I'd be very flaterd. I've always had a crush on you. I think you are the prittyest lady I have ever seen in my life. I espeshily love your eyelashes. And your lips ah... they are as red as butuful leaves in the Fall.
Love,
William Shakespeare
P.S. I will pick you up at 7:00 tonight and we will dance under the moonlight until our hearts content!

Brittany Shaw (age 7)

Alicia Buck (age 7)

Anne had noticed William too; they often saw each other,
And soon the couple knew that they were meant for one another.

Dear William,
Yes I will go out with you
tonight. All I need is time
with you. Your eyes glitter
like stars. Your dazzling
clothes are magnifisint
We could have a great
fyoucher. We'll have lots of
children. William Shakespeare
I admire you with glee.
                    Your honey
                         Annie

Alex Woodley (age 8)

Marijke Altenburg (age 7)

He asked her for her hand and she agreed with blushing cheeks,
And they were married quietly in just a few short weeks.

The Dream Girl

William told his mom he was going on a date. His dad said "WOO LOVER BOY." Later that day, he knocked at the Hathaway's door to pick up Annie. They stroled throo the Avon Park and after a while William gave her a sweet kiss on the lips. He asked romantickly "Can you marry me?" "Yes I will dear loveing Shakespeare" gasped Annie.

Michael Piccolo (age 7)

Matt Charbonneau (age 7)

28

The Bishop signed the papers back in 1582.
And so they were united with the simple words, "I do."

Today William Shakespeare proudly walked down the aisle with his weded wife Anne Hathaway. The gown she wore was sparkling and flashing in the sunlight. It was a beautiful sight to see. And he was dressed in silk finery. That too was a magnifisent sight. He was 18 and she was 26!

Picture and story : Dulcie Vousden (age 7)

29

Their married life was quickly blessed; things could not stay the same,
For Anne soon had a baby girl; Susanna was her name.

Kimberly Brown (age 7)

William and Anne Shakespeare are prowd to present their new doter, Susanna Shakespeare. She was born in their bedroom on Henley Street at 12:00 am. She weighed in at 6.13 pownds and is a bowncing good baby, a real cutey!

Adam Robinson (age 8)

A few years later Anne had twins, to William's great delight:
Hamnet Shakespeare; Judith too, a sweet and joyous sight.

By the way the marriage was a huge sikses! They had three babies Susanna, Hamnet and Judith. William was out of his mind with amazemint! He was like a firecraker popping to the ceiling with joy. His babies were like little angels drifting in cradles of love!

*Ellen Stuart
(age 7)*

Hamnet   Judith

*Brittany Shaw
(age 7)*

31

William was enchanted; they were precious as could be.
He held his babies gently as he rocked them on his knee.

*Caitlin More
(age 7)*

The big day !

"I sit in my rocker near the fire singing my babies to sleep while Susanna plays on the floor. How <u>excited</u> I am. A smile crosses Hamnet's face. Judith slowly closes her eyes with Hamnet following. For you see, Anne has just had twins, a day old already but still very sleepy. As I gaze down at my tired babies, I realize how <u>lucky</u> I am. Twins, I have twins!"

William

*Katie
Brown
(age 7)*

Now all these kids were stuffed into the home of William's dad;
This overcrowded house was simply driving William mad.

Feb. 1585

Dear Diary,
Now we have three children and 12 people living in my father's house and how crowded it is. There are people bumping into each other, babies crying, and there's never any peace and quiet. I think if another person sets a foot into this house it will icsplode! All this comoshon is driving me nuts. I can't even hear myself think. I need a brake!

William Shakespeare

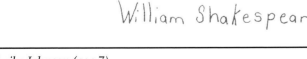

Anika Johnson (age 7)

*Julie Wilhelm
(age 8))*

Soon William went to London where his fortune could be made.
Though he missed his wife and kids, the trip just couldn't be delayed.

Jo-Jeff Dunbar (age 8)

London was a city full of life and spirit too.
William looked for work, although the jobs around were few.

Now theatre was growing to some new and splendid heights,
Despite the fact that certain people frowned upon these sights.

Robyn Lafontaine (age 7)

William Shakespeare
London England

1p
Queen ElizaBeth

To Anne Shakespeare
Henley Street
Stratford - upon - Avon
England

London England,
June 1587

Dear Annie,

I really miss you and the kids but I think coming to London was the right desishon. I am amazed at how huge London is, way biger than Stratford. When I went over London Bridge the view took my breth away. The sun was just going down and the colers were spiktaculer. There are three theatres here The Rose, The Theatre and The Curtain. I'm hoping I get a job at one of them tomorow. Give the kids a hug for me. I'll be back on the weekend.

Love to you all
William S.

Amberly Henry (age 7)

So William started slowly as a call or water boy;
He always worked his hardest but these jobs held little joy.

Dear Anne,

I now have a job as a call boy at the theatre. It can be very frusterating moving props. You need a lot of breath and a fast pace to run on and off the stage. It's allways push and shuv. I even get treated like a prop. Say hi to mother, father and the kids for me.

Your beloved,
William

Marijke Altenburg (age 7)

Robert Stroh (age 8)

Then he became an actor with a fine, dramatic flair;
William took on many roles and his talents he did share.

Waiting for my cue...
Stomach **shivering**
Legs **shaking,**
On I charge
Bursts of laughter,
Loud chuckles from the audience
Such a gratifying sound,
So proud
To be an actor!

William Shakespeare
London England

Julian Smith (age 7)

Kate Bean
(age 7)

He adored this way of life, but his work was rather brief
The deadly plague hit London bringing many people grief.

The English did not know what was the cause of this disease,
They stayed within their houses, hoping God would hear their pleas.

Ashley Kropf (age 9)

June 1592 ... all the theatres have been closed.
My dreams for acting have crumbled beneath my
fingers. I'm stuck at home pacing. Si yantists do not
have the slitest idea how the deadly dizees
spreads itself. Many people fear from the sickness
that may be here for senchuries. We all fear
the powerful sign of death.

William

Ella Fox (age 7)

For two long years, the theatres were silent, dark and cold,
And William wrote some poems which he found were quickly sold.

Venus and Adonis

William was a hard working man indeed. He spent weeks and years writing his plays. William had a tuff time with the kids climbing on his desk and whining in his ear. But it was all worth it. His plays were spicktakuler!

Michael Piccolo (age 7)

Kelly Ehgoetz, (age 7)

That second year, at Christmastime, a present came Will's way;
He'd been commissioned by the Queen to come perform a play.

Dec. 5, 1594

Dear William Shakespeare,

Me and my ladys in waiting would like to invite you and your ackting groop to do 2 plays for me at my palase. Please pik 2 of your very best! We deeply think your acktors and espesheley you William Shakespeare are the greatest in all of England.

Love,
Queen Elizabeth

P.S. Make shur you are here on Dec. 26 at 1:00 on the dot! After the play we will have roste pig and froot salid!

Lauren Vancea (age 7)

Dulcie Vousden (age 7)

And so to Greenwich Palace, William set off at quick speed.
He showed his play to all the court, a fine and honoured deed.

The Queen was just ecstatic with the work that Will had done.
It seemed that all of William's happy fortunes had begun.

Robyn Lafontaine (age 7)

Dec. 27, 1594

Dear Anne,
You won't beleve who I met. Her majisty, Queen Elizabeth invited me to her house. Greenwich Palace is enormus. There was gold and silver everywhere. I just stared in amazement. The Lord Chamberlain was there too. I was so tense when we put on my play but when I herd the Queen giggling I felt as proud as could be. Elizabeth is not what I expekted. She was dressed quite well. She had the bigest farthingale I've ever seen. She had firey red hair tied up in a bun. It was a fantastic day!
Sinserly,
William

Alex Woodley (age 8)

41

His luck continued through the years until one stormy eve
Young Hamnet died, a tragic loss, his family left to grieve.

His son was just eleven when he left his earthly frame;
He was buried 'neath a headstone which was printed with his name.

Picture: Brittany Shaw (age 7)
Caption: Jeff Brown (age 7)

My little angel is gone. I wish I had him back
even for two hours. I want to say good-bye.

Poor William was a broken man and felt an aching loss;
He knelt and wept in sorrow at his son's secluded cross.

Robyn Lafontaine,
(age 7)

My only son Hamnet is dead.
It can't be troo. Why did he
leve me? Let my garden die. Let
my life die... But not Hamnet.
My hart is broken. God take
care of him!

Marijke
Altenburg
(age 7)

43

The next few years continued at a rather quiet pace.
Then in 1597, William Shakespeare bought "New Place."

The dwelling was impressive, and it stood on Chapel Street
Though for William, without Hamnet, success was bittersweet.

Jo-Jeff Dunbar (age 8)

But time is the great healer and he slowly felt renewed;
William focussed on his work and regained a happy mood.

He turned back to his poetry, his vivid lines of thought.
He immersed himself in words and the dreams that he once sought.

Dulcie
Vousden
(age 7)

But an actor and a writer must also have a stage.
The theatres in London town were all the current rage.

Since there was no place to rent William built one of his own;
He cherished this new playhouse; The Globe as it was known.

The Globe was open to the sky, so plays were in the day.
The poor folk stood about the stage; a penny they did pay.

Ashley Kropf (age 9)

They were labelled "groundlings" and could get quite loud and rude;
If they didn't like the play they saw, they'd even throw their food.

Others paid a good deal more for shelter from the rain.
 But on opening day for Shakespeare, not one person did complain.

Brad Jesson
(age 7)

Alex Woodley
(age 8)

London, England [1599]

Dear Anne,
Today was the grand opening of my Globe. I had a bad case of buterflys in my stumic. The Globe looked so large and I felt so small. But when I went on stage my buterflys floo away At the end of the play the crowd clapt so loud it sounded like an earthquake. Even the groundlings loved it. I didn't see any tomatos. Anne this is one of the happyest days of my life!

William

Sometimes he wrote great tragedies, like *Hamlet* and *Macbeth*,
That told of trial and misery while weeping over death.

Ashley Kropf (age 9)

Kimberly Brown (age 8)

He also wrote some comedies and plays about the past;
The many kings of England were quite often in his cast.

*Adam Robinson
(age 7)*

*Julian Hacquebard
(age 7)*

*Laura Bates
(age 6)*

When the good Queen died at seventy in the year 1603,
The new king, James, paid William for more plays that all could see.

The Comedy of Errors

King Lear

Measure for Measure

Othello

As You Like It

Coriolanus

Julie Wilhelm, (age 8)

I would like to write plays like Shakespeare.
I can just see it in my little brain and
pounding hart. I would be famis!

Matthew Doughty (age 7)

He dubbed the troupe "The King's Men" and lent them his support.
Then William and his partners were invited to his court.

The palace was called Whitehall; they performed there quite a lot.
'Twas near 200 times, in fact, their acting skills were sought.

Amberly Henry (age 7)

They also triumphed at the Globe; their group achieved much fame.
In London, William Shakespeare had become a household name.

Dear Anne

My play Henry the Fifth was a hit! It was a thrill being in front of all those people. It was simply marvilis. The crowd was cheering like elifants rampaging. It was so loud it hurt my ears. Even the groundlings liked it. I have a sore back from all the bowing!

William

Carl Leushuis (age 7)

Ryan Flanagan (age 9)

Ella Fox (age 7)

Dear Anney,

My play AS YOU LIKE IT was on. Teers spred from my face. The crowd clapt like thunder and cheered oh so lowd. Tiny wislls could be heard. Roses were tossed on to the stage. King James was tickled pink!

Your loved one,
William Shakespeare

The English people liked Will's plays; his works were well received.
They flocked to William's theatre to watch the tales he weaved.

A happy smile lit up his face, for things were going well.
It seemed all London was enthralled by Will's dramatic spell.

Michael Chambers (age 8)

Yet life did not leave William with his happiness for long.
The winds of fate were whipping up another mournful song.

The warm June day was grim when William saw the ashes fall
Upon the grave of what had been his dearest dream of all.

Ian Clark
(age 9)

The Globe was putting on a play when things were set awry.
A small cannon had been fired that sent cinders to the sky.

They fell upon the thatch, which had formed a partial roof,
And William's treasured theatre exploded with a poof.

Mike Williams (age 7)

His eyes grew wide in horror as a single fiery gust,
Snatched up his Globe in burning hands and crushed it into dust.

Matt Charbonneau (age 7)

> June 29, 1613
>
> Dear Anney
> My masterpece the globe has brnt to Ashis. I feel like Hamnet has died again.
> I am in the depths of despair. Tell the kids I will be late coming home tonight. This has been a day of horer.
>
>   Your beLoved
>   William

Ella Fox (age 7)

> June 29, 1613
>
> Dear Anne
> I have some dredful noos for you Anne. Our Globe Theatre is histery! Gone capush! A spark hit the roof and our glorius theatre was brnt to smithereens. My life is rooind. I won't be home tonight dear. I'm too sad hunny!
>   Love your misrabl Shakespeare
>   Boo hoo

Marijke Altenburg (age 7)

William's heart was broken though no mortal blood was spilled.
His dreams now lay in ashes, and his spirit had been killed.

Tom
Landers
(age 7)

He slipped back to his quiet home and lived his final years,
Recalling all that was his life, his happiness and tears.

Dulcie Vousden (age 7)

William's 52nd birthday is recorded as his last;
On that sad day all Stratford mourned. The flags were at half-mast.

April 23, 1616

Today my father died. I was down by the Avon river waching the waves. It was Strange...the river moaned and then groo still and I Knew Something was wrong. I lisined for the wisper of the wind but again I feared the worst. I paniced and ran for home. My mother told me the teribil news. A river of tears rolled down my cheeks and fell to the floor. I have lost a magnifisent dad. The world has lost a genyus!

Susanna Shakespeare

Brittany Shaw (age 7)

Ashley Kropf (age 9)

'Twas in the Church of Trinity, dear Will was laid to rest,
And of this loss a friend of his most surely said it best:

"The Avon wept a thousand tears without her loving friend;
The very flowers hung their heads as though it were the end."

Dulcie Vousden
(age 7)

Yes, at that time, Will's gentle soul did mark its final page.
The curtain closed, and William Shakespeare exited the stage.

Jenny Geoghegan (age 8)

Although the Bard's life now is but an echo from the past,
His words are with us still today and will forever last.

*Karolyn
Gagnier
(age 9)*

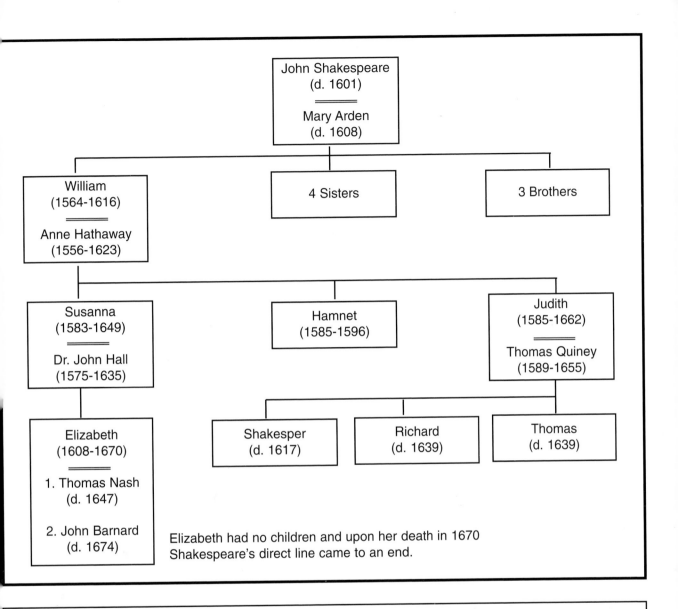

```
                    ┌─────────────────────┐
                    │  John Shakespeare    │
                    │     (d. 1601)        │
                    │  ═══════════════     │
                    │    Mary Arden        │
                    │     (d. 1608)        │
                    └─────────────────────┘
```

John Shakespeare
(d. 1601)
══════════
Mary Arden
(d. 1608)

William
(1564-1616)
══════════
Anne Hathaway
(1556-1623)

4 Sisters

3 Brothers

Susanna
(1583-1649)
══════════
Dr. John Hall
(1575-1635)

Hamnet
(1585-1596)

Judith
(1585-1662)
══════════
Thomas Quiney
(1589-1655)

Elizabeth
(1608-1670)
══════════
1. Thomas Nash
(d. 1647)

2. John Barnard
(d. 1674)

Shakesper
(d. 1617)

Richard
(d. 1639)

Thomas
(d. 1639)

Elizabeth had no children and upon her death in 1670
Shakespeare's direct line came to an end.

I think Shakespeare had a brain from god. His brain was as smart as life and is for always!

Devon Searle (age 7)

Parents and Educators

Most students will be exposed to Shakespeare at some point in their educational careers. Traditionally, this initial exposure has been delayed until their high school years. When I set out to write this book, I wanted to share the excitement of exploring with children of all ages the timeless emotions of Shakespeare. For the children, Shakespeare became a friend, not someone to be feared. Here are a few suggestions you might find helpful as you share this book with your children.

- Use the poem as a basis for a play on the life of William Shakespeare.

- Research how people lived in Elizabethan times.

- Use globes and maps to locate Shakespeare's birthplace.

- Trace the routes he might have taken in Stratford-upon-Avon.

- Conduct interviews, role-playing the parts of the reporter and Shakespeare.

- Explore the feelings of Shakespeare through the writing of diaries and letters.

- Construct models of the Globe Theatre.

- Celebrate Shakespeare's birthday on April 23.

Above, *Josh Dale, 7, Kristy Brandon, 7, Kelly Elder, 7, Kate Landreth, 7, Gavin Vanderwater, 7 display their work in Lois's classroom.*

Educators who wish to stage performances of *A Child's Portrait of Shakespeare* should contact the author to request permission:

Fax: (519) 273-0712
E-mail: lburdett@shakespearecanbefun.com

Right,*Gavin Vanderwater, 7, and Kate Landreth, 7, reenact the life of William Shakespeare.*